Christmas in Williamsburg

Christmas in Williamsburg

Photographs by
TAYLOR BIGGS LEWIS, JR.

Text by
JOANNE B. YOUNG

THE COLONIAL WILLIAMSBURG FOUNDATION
Williamsburg, Virginia

Distributed by
HOLT, RINEHART AND WINSTON, INC.
New York

Library of Congress Catalogue Card Number: 79-122942

Holt, Rinehart and Winston SBN:
  03-085320-6 (Trade)
Colonial Williamsburg SBN:
  910412-85-5 (Trade), 910412-84-7 (Trade paper)

   Photographs on pages 32, 38, 39, and 49 courtesy
of *Better Homes and Gardens Christmas Ideas*, © 1966
by Meredith Corporation, all rights reserved.

PRINTED IN THE UNITED STATES OF AMERICA

WOOD smoke drifts upward in the blue frosty air, a pungent perfume older than the eighteenth-century ceremony about to begin. Approaching footsteps can be heard—skipping, tap-tapping, scuffling, striding—as all along Duke of Gloucester Street and the little paths winding from Francis and Nicholson Streets, townspeople and visitors converge on the Capitol.

As Williamsburg honored a great victory, a peace treaty, or the birthday of a sovereign in colonial times, today the Christmas season will be ushered in with a Grand Illumination of the town to celebrate the birth of the Infant King.

5

Bonfires in front of the brick wall surrounding the building draw the crowd like magnets. The people warm their hands and then their backsides as sparks fly upward in a cheery celebration of their own. Just above the historic Capitol's cupola the white moon rides in the December sky, a fitting celestial illumination.

"Here comes the Militia!" someone calls, and an excited child spots the drummers assembling. The Captain of the Militia leads his men forward to dip their torches into the bonfire, orange-gold flames punctuating the night with excitement. Others march into view carrying candle-lighted lanthorns.

Now the rousing music of the Fifes and Drums grows nearer; and the Night Watch, holding his lanthorn high, takes his place at the head of the march.

"Joy to the world," sing the sharp-voiced fifes. "The Lord is come," reply the deep-throated drums.

The torchlit column of militiamen forms up smartly, followed by the young scarlet-coated musicians; and hundreds of enthusiastic spectators fall in behind.

"Mr. Marot, Mr. Burdett—light your candles!" commands the Night Watch; and in Marot's and Burdett's ordinaries, where many a cup of cheer was raised in Christmases past, white candles wink on in every window.

"Mistress Hunter, Mr. Wetherburn—light your candles!" The darkened windows of the Millinery Shop and the tavern promptly glow.

Down the mile-long street that once knew the steps of young Mr. Jefferson and Colonel George Washington, wise George Wythe and elegant Colonel William Byrd, they march, transforming the black winter night into twinkling squares of yellow candlelight. Now the windows of shops, homes, taverns, the Courthouse, the Printing Office and beloved Bruton Parish Church shine as they did on great occasions two centuries ago.

At last the marchers reach the Wren Building, venerable heart of the College of William and Mary, and stop at the door of the President's House where Dr. Davis Y. Paschall greets them.

he glow of a bonfire turns the Capitol's windows to gold
s the moon joins in the Grand Illumination.

Carrying their torches high, the Militia lead the nighttime march down Duke of Gloucester Street, candles winking on in every window as they pass.

"It seems especially appropriate that the Grand Illumination should conclude on this sacred ground," he tells them, "for it was here that the early patriots studied and formed the concepts that were translated into the great documents undergirding our republic."

Just as his colonial predecessors may have done, he then reads from St. Luke: "And suddenly there was with the angels a multitude of the heavenly host, praising God and saying, 'Glory to God in the highest, and on earth peace, good will toward men.'"

Then the president gives them his greetings in words said to have been written by an Italian poet, Fra Giovanni, nearly one-hundred years before the first English settlers landed at Jamestown:

> No heaven can come to us unless our hearts
>> Find rest in today. Take Heaven!
> No peace lies in the future which is not hidden
>> In this present little instant. Take Peace!
> The gloom of the world is but a shadow.
>> Behind it, yet within our reach, is Joy.
> There is radiance and glory in the darkness,
>> Could we but see; and to see, we have only to look.
> I beseech you to look.

Hundreds of eyes look back down Duke of Gloucester Street whose darkness is now so radiant, and Christmas has begun in Colonial Williamsburg.

In the snow-hushed streets at twilight, a young woman in her scarlet cloak seems part of some merry Christmas two centuries ago.

9

Simple garlands and wreaths of pine decorate the tiny Isham Goddin House on Waller Street.

WHAT were they like—those early Christmases when Williamsburg was young, a lusty, dusty growing town not "quaint" but contemporary; not so much "pretty" as vital? Certainly they were different from those of the present.

No Santa Claus was part of colonial folklore. Gifts were limited to tokens of appreciation to servants on the day after Christmas—St. Stephen's Day—and occasional remembrances to children on New Year's.

The custom of the Christmas tree did not make its way from Germany to Williamsburg until 1842. That year a young teacher at the College of William and Mary, Charles Minnigerode, decorated a tree as it was done in his homeland for the children of his friend, Professor Nathaniel Beverley Tucker, in their home on Market Square.

Decorations in homes and shops, where they appeared at all, were far simpler than ours, and so were their festivities. The gaiety,

More elaborate wreaths on Williamsburg doors today still use only the natural materials—like bayberry, fruit, and pine cones—available when the colonial capital was young.

however, was just as genuine as it is today when year-round eighteenth-century amusements are compressed into two gala weeks for visitors. It is, perhaps, the very simplicity of colonial life that is the most appealing, along with what John Bernard, an English visitor, called "their conviviality," which was "like their summers, as radiant as it was warm."

"Nothing is now to be heard of in conversation, but the Balls, the Fox-hunts, the fine entertainments, and the good fellowship, which are to be exhibited at the approaching Christmas," wrote Philip Fithian in his journal the week before Christmas, 1773. Fithian was tutor for the younger children of Robert Carter of Nomini Hall —seventeen in all, six of whom were born while the family resided in Williamsburg.

For tutors like Fithian, it was hard to keep order in the classroom when thoughts of the holidays ahead filled their pupils' minds. William and Mary turned loose its students in the grammar school, the

The brass finial on the railing before the Millinery Shop sparkles in a nest of Christmas greens.

In the little garden building of the Brush-Everard House,
wreath-making is the order of the day.

Indian school, and the college from December 16 until January 6. Some found it hard to wait for the official closing, however, and in schools and on plantations evoked the English custom of "barring out" their professors in hopes of starting the holiday sooner. Sometimes they succeeded!

Such merriment as the observant Fithian noted was not unusual

The traditional nineteenth-century Christmas tree in the central gallery of the Abby Aldrich Rockefeller Folk Art Collection.

in the hospitable Old Dominion where the Christmas season offered a perfect opportunity for family reunions, feasts, and balls. Twelve days of Christmas were hardly long enough to catch up on the news, the gossip, the price of tobacco and corn, the exchange of views on the latest London styles and local politics.

Christmas visits were, in fact, the satisfactory substitute for telegraph, television, and telephone—the moment of warm communication which melted time and distance between isolated communities and welded the bonds of blood and friendship. It was a time for courting, for weddings, and for the renewal of family ties. (George Washington and Martha Custis were married on Twelfth Day in 1759, and Thomas Jefferson took Martha Skelton as his bride on New Year's Day, 1772.)

The winter season in the colony, and later in the commonwealth, was a relaxed one for the most part.

Under the kissing ball,
a man and a maid put
mistletoe to its best
time-honored use.

15

Like some ancient piece of sculpture, the paper mulberry tree at the Robert Carter House is a study in winter serenity.

16

*The centuries meet as a hostess in eighteenth-century dress
and her blue-jeaned daughter stroll by the Printing Office.*

*Icicles fringe the eaves, and snow frosts
the fenceposts and roofs of houses and shops.*

*Two cardinals and a sparrow enjoy
their own Christmas feast.*

18

The doorway of the Ludwell-Paradise House wears a fan of apples centered on a pineapple, the colonial symbol of hospitality.

At the Sign of the Golden Ball, the watchmaker helps a lady up the snowy steps as James Craig may have welcomed customers on a winter's day.

WILLIAMSBURG shopkeepers and craftsmen had until April to replenish their stocks for the frantically busy period when the General Court was in session again and Publick Times began. Until then the town's population would remain at no more than two thousand, an equal number of temporary residents having made their way homeward after the fall session was over.

Dull the quiet streets might seem by comparison—no fairs crowding Market Square, few traveling players performing at the theatre—but there was time enough (and room) for a lively game of draughts or dice at one of the taverns, or a leisurely pint of ale or mug of grog to warm a man on his way home from work.

For merchants and planters alike, the holiday from Christmas until Twelfth Night ("Old Christmas") was one of the most festive seasons of the year, with hearty eating and drinking the order of the day.

A cat climbs to the ridgepole of a shingle roof, ignoring the snow and daintily keeping her feet dry.

Pine garlands, pyracantha, and pine cones festoon the entrance to the Raleigh Tavern.

21

The Raleigh Tavern's small dining room is decked with
Christmas finery—apple cones on the sideboard; and bayberry, holly,
and lady apples nestled in cedar on the table.

Wetherburn's Tavern, famous for its
arrack punch, no doubt echoed to
hundreds of holiday toasts served
from the Wassail Bowl.

While fences and fields were capped with snow, the kitchen became the hub of domestic activity. The Palace kitchen holds spicy aromas of all the delights of a colonial gourmet's feast.

ON nearby plantations like Carter's Grove, the barns were full and the tobacco cured. While fields were soggy with early winter rains or furrows were ridged with snow, outdoor work was limited to taking care of the stock and chopping wood—prodigious amounts of it to stoke the hungry fires for heating and cooking.

Trading ships had set sail down the James for England or the West Indies, their holds filled with the year's crop of grain, tobacco,

or barrel staves; and the fate of their cargo was now in the lap of the gods and the London factors.

The man of the family, from planter to craftsman, freeholder to field hand, could pull up his chair by the fire, rest his boots on the fender, and light his clay pipe while he indulged in satisfaction with the year just past, or hope for the coming spring.

If it had been a good year, fragrant cured hams and lean sides of

Are holiday guests arriving? A hostess watches through the swirling snow from the stairway of the Peyton Randolph House as Mistress Randolph may have done.

bacon hung in the smokehouse. Peanuts and chestnuts were ready for roasting; and plump potatoes, turnips, and apples in their baskets lined the walls of cool storerooms. Barrels of corn and wheat were sufficient, with the miller's help, to provide bread for the long winter. Bottles of good wine told of a plentiful harvest from the vineyard.

In Williamsburg kitchens, from the elegant Palace to the simpler homes of the gunsmith and silversmith, herbs had been hung to dry along with strings of onions and precious lemons from Lisbon.

Even the lady of the house could fall into a simpler routine than in the autumn days when sweet gum trees turned gold and geese flew south in V-shaped flocks. Then the garden's bounty had meant long days of filling her larder for winter, and supervising the spinning, weaving, and sewing of warm clothing for the chilly days ahead.

Now these tasks were behind them, and Christmas—that happy season—was ahead.

As the *Virginia Almanack* for 1766 advised:

> Now Christmas comes, 'tis fit that we
> Should feast and sing, and merry be:
> Keep open house, let fidlers play,
> A fig for cold, sing care away;
> And may they who thereat repine,
> On brown bread and on small beer dine.

The rhymester's advice was well heeded. From the simplest Williamsburg house to the most magnificent plantation, Christmas was kept in its own fashion.

*Christmas in Williamsburg has always been a season for
happy homecomings like this one at the Brush-Everard House.*

On Christmas Eve Williamsburg's visitors and townspeople gather for the lighting of the community tree near the Powder Magazine in Market Square.

CHRISTMAS DAY itself was primarily a holy day, with the entire family making its way on foot, on horseback, or by carriage to the parish church. Servants were given the day off from their labors to attend services also.

Bruton Parish Church was festively decorated at Christmas throughout the colonial period. Bishop Francis M. Whittle wrote to the rector in 1879: "The decoration of the Church building being a custom as old as the Church itself in Virginia, may lawfully and properly be continued."

28

▶

On the holy day that marks the Infant's birth, the sacraments are given as they have been for two and a half centuries.

The bell in Bruton Parish Church spire joyously peals its call to worship.

In the sanctuary, the scent of pine mingled with the aroma of bayberry candles as the silver communion cup, the church's most priceless possession, was passed to worshipers. Heads bowed in prayer, hearts lifted in praise, they gave thanks for the recurring miracle of the birth of the Holy Child.

Decorating their churches with garlands of greens for the holiday followed the admonition of an old English rhyme:

> Holly and ivy, box and bay,
> Put in the church on Christmas Day.

All of these could be gathered abundantly by children or servants in the forests around Williamsburg as the festive day approached.

At the Red Lion (a colonial inn with "very good accommodations for Man and Horse," now a private home) spruce garlands are looped to the banister. At the landing balustrade, magnolia leaves cover a plaque centered with pomegranates, grapes, Seckel pears, and Jerusalem cherries.

30

Heap on more wood!—the wind is chill;
But let it whistle as it will
We'll keep our Christmas merry still.

SIR WALTER SCOTT

*As he passes the Nicolson Shop on snowy
Duke of Gloucester Street, the craftsman on his
way to work might echo these words.*

So could mistletoe, by those nimble enough to climb a tree, tall
enough to reach for it, or good enough marksmen to shoot it down.
According to a popular Norse legend, the glistening green plant
with its white berries could not only command a kiss but brought
luck and fertility as well. Tiny sprigs of it were sometimes tucked
into invitations to gala parties to wish each guest happiness and
prosperity in the coming year.

Other greens native to the Virginia countryside were probably
also used to "deck the halls": pine, waxy magnolia leaves, soft red
cedar, rosemary, and cherry laurel.

A pyramid of fruit makes a sparkling table centerpiece . . .

. . . while a louvered door holds a wreath of magnolia leaves, artfully decorated with pineapple halves, dried okra pods, pine cones, boxwood, lemons, apples, oranges, limes, and pears.

A pair of duck decoys in a centerpiece at the Red Lion reflects the feeling of the old English print above the sideboard.

PRINTS contemporary to the decades in which Williamsburg was the colonial capital show many artistic arrangements of fruit suitable for gracing Christmas tables, mantels, and entry halls at the holiday season.

Did Mistress Everard, Mistress Reynolds, Mistress Randolph and other Williamsburg ladies decorate their doorways as modern residents do? We do not know. No reference has been found to this practice in surviving diaries, letters, or newspapers. Beginning in a much earlier period, a wide variety of greens were used in England to decorate homes, shops, and churches during the Christmas season. Since most Virginians before the Revolutionary War considered them-

A couple make their way up the lanthorn-bordered walk to the Governor's Palace, where candlelight concerts add their music to the Christmas season.

selves English and observed many of the customs of their homeland, it is reasonable to expect that this holiday tradition was also carried out by at least some of them. If she were decorating the inside of her home with greens, an imaginative Williamsburg lady might also have created a decoration for her front door—but this is only speculative.

From the pine wreaths in shop windows to the garlands on the Palace balustrade, decorations today express the spirit of those earlier times. They contain only the natural materials (fruits, nuts, greens, cones, or seed pods) that were available to the housewife of two hundred years ago. Sprigs of holly are tucked behind old English prints and mirrors on the walls in the eighteenth-century manner,

*Double doors call for
twin arrangements of lemons . . .*

*. . . while the Millinery Shop is
adorned with a wreath of pine
cones, holly, bayberry, and
cotton pod "stars."*

massed around pewter plates, or used to encircle punch bowls in homes and taverns.

Other decorations may be arranged in a Chinese porcelain bowl, a delicate creamware epergne, even a mahogany tea caddy—for the nature of woman has changed little over the years in which her fashions have ranged from farthingales to pants suits. A hostess of any day has wanted to "put her best foot forward" by making her home its most beautiful when guests were expected. And she has used her ingenuity to create that beauty from the objects she had at hand.

A blue and white china bowl in the entry hall of the George Wythe House holds white pine, magnolia leaves, holly, and cedar—and cotton bolls white as the snow outside.

As their colonial predecessors may have done, today's homemakers in Williamsburg create imaginative arrangements of berries, nuts, cones, and fruit like this one in an antique tea caddy at the Powell-Waller House, a private home.

36

The feast of Christmas seems about to begin as the candles
are lighted in the Brush-Everard dining room, its table centered with
an apple cone copied from an eighteenth-century print.

Nandina, cedar, and pittosporum are gracefully combined in a brass compote at the Benjamin Waller House, a private Williamsburg residence.

Fruit, greens, and cones form an elegant "Hogarth curve" for the centerpiece at the Waller House, while candles add their glow to a companion arrangement on the buffet.

A pine wreath at the window and the punch bowl ringed with apples and holly, hospitable Wetherburn's Tavern awaits the arrival of yuletide guests.

CHRISTMAS came to Virginia in the damp, crowded holds of tiny sailing ships, packed in somewhere between the tools and precious nails, the seeds and the family treasures. Its spirit first arrived in Jamestown with the *Susan Constant*, the *Discovery*, and the *Godspeed*, which put out from London down the Thames River five days before Christmas in 1606. The following December, snow and freezing winds kept Captain John Smith and a band of his men in a Kecoughtan village, where Powhatan's friendly Indians prepared a Christmas feast for them: "We were never more merrie nor fedde on more plentie of good oysters, fish, flesh, wild foule, and good bread." The tradition of hospitality evidently goes back to the original Virginians!

In 1649 Henry Norwood, bound for the Old Dominion in the *Virginia Merchant*, recorded in his diary how steadily the small flame of Christmas burned in even the dire circumstances surrounding those almost-starving voyagers:

> Many sorrowful days and nights were spun out in this manner, till the blessed feast of Christmas came upon us, which we began with a very melancholy solemnity; and yet, to make some distinction of times, the scrapings of the meal-tubs were all amassed together to compose a pudding. Malaga sack, sea water, with fruit and spice, all well fryed in oil, were the ingredients of this regale, which raised some envy in the spectators; but allowing some privilege to the captain's mess, we met no obstruction, but did peaceably enjoy our Christmas pudding.

The yule log is brought in with much ceremony, holly placed on top to kindle the fire.

*In the Great Hall of the Wren Building, visitors at the
annual yule reception toss a sprig of holly on the blazing yule log,
in the old English custom, to burn up their troubles of the past year.*

As dusk falls, the lamplighter at the Governor's Palace follows a time-honored routine, spilling a pool of golden light through the winter dusk.

The banner in front of Christiana Campbell's Tavern was never truer than at Christmas time.

BY the eighteenth century, life was far easier for the Virginia colonists; and the *Virginia Almanack*, published in Williamsburg, could poetically describe the season:

> Christmas is come, hang on the pot,
> Let spits turn round, and ovens be hot;
> Beef, pork, and poultry, now provide
> To feast thy neighbours at this tide;
> Then wash all down with good wine and beer
> And so with mirth conclude the YEAR.

Williamsburg ovens were indeed hot and the spits turning! From them came succulent dishes for its "groaning boards"—tables that all but groaned under the weight of their steaming dishes, with sometimes an echoing groan from diners after too much feasting.

A silver punch bowl at the Peyton Randolph House gleams with mellow reflections of its wreath of fruit— and Christmases past.

*Belsnickel (Nicholas in Furs), the Pennsylvania Dutch figure
of the Christ Child's helper—giver of gifts to good children and switches
to bad ones—presides over a modern party table at the Norton-Cole House.*

45

The table in the dining room of the James Geddy House—eighteenth-century home of James Geddy, Jr., silversmith—is set with a delft soup tureen and decorated with four bands of fruit, pine cones, and cranberries.

For generations hospitality has been
the hallmark of Carter's Grove
plantation on the James River, southeast
of Williamsburg. A kissing ball hangs
in the pantry window.

To the delight of children a Victorian
Christmas tree stands each year in the
wide paneled entrance hall, decorated
with popcorn strings, cookies, and
treasured old ornaments.

48

In the plantation kitchen polished red apples in a wooden bowl, gingerbread men from the Raleigh Tavern Bakery, and tendrils of ivy all say "Merry Christmas."

In the stately dining room of Carter's Grove, the table is set in the colonial manner for the first course of dishes—an elegant array of sirloin of beef, artichokes in tomato aspic, cranberry relish, roast wild turkey, scalloped oysters, and petit pois in rings of acorn squash.

ND what a temptation was offered to the gourmet's palate: creamy peanut soup, fragrant baked ham, succulent scalloped oysters, roast wild turkey, roast beef—that delight of any true Englishman—crusty game pie with tender pheasant, fresh mushrooms and celery laced with a white wine sauce, Sally Lunn and spoon bread topped with butter, sweet potatoes baked in their jackets, plum puddings, Tipsy Squire, spicy mince pies, and fruit cakes studded with jewels of candied fruit. Then to wash it all down there was syllabub, mulled cider, Madeira, dark beer, or punch (which from their recipes sound potent enough to curl a wig!).

At the George Wythe House, a tempting dish of marzipan and crystallized ginger.

Holiday goodies fit for a royal governor are festively displayed in the small dining room of the Palace. At center, a pecan pie and fruit ambrosia; atop the tiered plate, a wine gelatin mold. Then (clockwise): a tree-shaped pastry, croquembouche de Noël; individual fruit cakes; plum pudding; petit fours; candied orange and lemon rinds and cherries; pecan and cherry tarts; a colonial fruit cake; and rum cream pie.

Wetherburn's Tavern glows with candlelight for Christmas guests. Music plays in the Great Room and cressets light up the courtyard behind the tavern.

T HE fare at Williamsburg holiday tables is one thing that has changed very little over the centuries. Visitors gather round "groaning boards" again. An especially elaborate feast at the King's Arms Tavern features that traditional showpiece of English Christmas dinners, the mock turtle arrangement of a calf's head, which is carried in on an elegantly decorated platter to the accompaniment of fifers. Here, as at Chowning's and Christiana Campbell's taverns, the holiday menu includes many favorite old Virginian delicacies. At private parties and in public dining rooms, an early Williamsburg citizen would feel much at home.

Fiddlers still play, and ballad singers beguile their listeners with the same songs—ribald or romantic—that won a cheer or a sentimental tear from eighteenth-century audiences.

Piping hot sugar wafers sizzle and steam as the eighteenth-century baking irons are put to use again at the Wetherburn kitchen.

A strolling minstrel at Chowning's Tavern sings for the diners a ballad of Christmas from colonial times.

For the "Crown of the Turtle" feast at the King's Arms, fifers announce the arrival of a galantine of calf's head. It is garnished with sweetbreads, artichokes du fond, veal birds, mushrooms, and truffles, and wears a forcemeat crown.

56

At the King's Arms, the ballad singer serenades a very young lady who finds his music even more fascinating than the food.

A colonial family would be quick to recognize, too, the volleys of musket fire and the boom of cannon in Market Square during the holiday season. From the early days in Jamestown (except in years when gunpowder was scarce and special laws forbade it) men would shoot their trusty flintlocks and sailors fired their ship's cannon as a salute to the season. The custom later evolved, in many parts of the South, into shooting firecrackers on Christmas Eve and Christmas morning. The revival of this tradition by the Militia is a popular one today, and fireworks add their brilliance to the New Year's Eve celebration, keeping both yuletide customs alive.

The guns of the Militia boom out in a holiday tradition older than the town itself, with the red-coated Fifes and Drums playing lively Christmas tunes as a prelude.

Colonial Sports Day is another event that has been revived, to the special enjoyment of children. "It will be our earnest endeavor," announces the master of ceremonies from his box alongside the eighteenth-century courthouse, "to provide you with certain innocent diversions in the form of games and sports familiar to any Virginian two hundred years ago." Market Square is a colorful sea of activity. There are hoop rolling, bag and foot racing, feats of strength, pitching quoits and pennies, bowling on the green, dancing, and the slippery contest to climb a "stout greased pole" for a bag of silver fastened to the top.

Colonial Sports Day is a highlight of the Christmas season for young visitors and for the Williamsburg children, in costumes of two centuries ago, who are ready to begin the hoop races.

"Three ladies of this city have baked a quantity of good fruit pies," announces the master of ceremonies, "and propose to determine those among you able to devour the greatest number in the shortest time."

Pinocchio and Geppetto cavort again on their miniature stage to the same delight of excited children that greeted the traveling puppeteer in colonial days.

AT the Abby Aldrich Rockefeller Folk Art Collection each holiday season brings new child-delighting displays of eighteenth- and nineteenth-century toys, along with special exhibits of twentieth-century origin. Unique hand-carved carrousel figures are on hand to be ridden—a giant rabbit, a giraffe, a pink pig, and a goat. Little girls especially love the Victorian doll house, complete with its own Christmas tree and tiny packages waiting to be opened by the doll children.

A tea party and a sleepy cat intrigue little girls under
the approving eye of a nineteenth-century miss on the gallery wall at
the Abby Aldrich Rockefeller Folk Art Collection.

A huge nineteenth-century Christmas tree takes the place of honor, decorated with gilded nuts, frosted animal-shaped ginger cookies, balls and dolls and Santa Clauses—some old, some new.

The cat on the carrousel must be patted before he is ridden.

" 'Tis the season to be jolly" sing the carolers at the Elizabeth Reynolds House, and music fills the frosty air.

ALONG the streets of the town, carolers bring the same happy fervor to "The Twelve Days of Christmas," "I Saw Three Ships A-Sailing In," and "God Rest ye Merry, Gentlemen" as songsters did two centuries ago. Music, in its timeless way, captures the spirit of the season at its best.

It is this spirit, most of all, which is to be found in Williamsburg at Christmas. It shines from candlelit windows, echoes in friendly footsteps down the cobble-edged streets, and is carried on the evening air in the mingled aroma of wood fires, baking gingerbread, and fresh-cut pine.

It is less to be found in sound than in silence, less to be talked about than treasured. And at its heart is the joy of it.